DATE DUE

COUNTRIES OF THE WORLD

Haiti

Gareth Stevens Publishing
A WORLD ALMANAC EDUCATION GROUP COMPANY

About the Author: Michele Wagner is a
graduate of California State University,
San Marcos. She works as a freelance writer
and editor and enjoys reading, cooking, and
traveling with her husband in her spare time.

Written by
MICHELE WAGNER

Edited by
PAUL ROZARIO

Edited in the U.S. by
MONICA RAUSCH
CATHERINE GARDNER

Designed by
JAILANI BASARI

Picture research by
SUSAN JANE MANUEL

First published in North America in 2002 by
Gareth Stevens Publishing
A World Almanac Education Group Company
330 West Olive Street, Suite 100
Milwaukee, Wisconsin 53212 USA

Please visit our web site at:
www.garethstevens.com
For a free color catalog describing
Gareth Stevens Publishing's list of high-quality
books and multimedia programs, call 1-800-542-2595
or fax your request to (414) 332-3567.

© TIMES MEDIA PRIVATE LIMITED 2002
Originated and designed by
Times Editions
An imprint of Times Media Private Limited
A member of the Times Publishing Group
Times Centre, 1 New Industrial Road
Singapore 536196
http://www.timesone.com.sg/te

Library of Congress Cataloging-in-Publication Data
Wagner, Michele.
Haiti / by Michele Wagner.
p. cm. — (Countries of the world)
Summary: Describes the geography, history,
government, economy, people, arts, social life,
and customs of the Caribbean country of Haiti.
Includes bibliographical references and index.
ISBN 0-8368-2351-6 (lib. bdg.)
1. Haiti—Juvenile literature. [1. Haiti.] I. Title.
II. Countries of the world (Milwaukee, Wis.)
F1915.2.W34   2002
972.94—dc21   2002017004

Printed in Malaysia

1 2 3 4 5 6 7 8 9 06 05 04 03 02

PICTURE CREDITS
AFP: 81
Michele Burgess: cover, 2, 3 (top), 16,
    34, 42, 43, 54, 60, 62
Camera Press: 15 (both), 48, 57, 66
    (right), 67
Eleanor Frank/Kay Shaw Photography:
    90 (both)
Getty Images/HultonArchive: 37,
    66 (left), 75, 76 (both), 77 (both),
    78, 79, 80 (bottom), 82, 84, 85
The Hutchison Library: 6 (bottom), 17,
    19, 38, 45, 55
Kay Shaw Photography: 6 (top), 24,
    28, 46, 47, 58, 59, 63
Earl Kowall: 32
Jason Laure: 13
North Wind Picture Archives: 52 (left),
    65, 68, 69
David Simson: 3 (center), 4, 5, 7, 22, 23,
    25, 29, 40, 41, 51, 52 (right), 56, 72,
    74, 91
Times Editions: 10, 11, 12 (both), 18,
    20 (both), 31, 33, 39, 44, 53, 64, 70
Topham Picturepoint: 3 (bottom), 9 (both),
    80 (top), 83
Mireille Vautier: 1, 8, 14, 21, 26, 27, 30,
    35, 36, 49, 50, 61, 71, 73, 87, 89

Digital Scanning by Superskill Graphics Pte Ltd

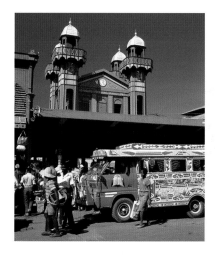

Contents

4

AN OVERVIEW OF HAITI

Haiti is a country of extremes, with dry, desertlike regions and rainy tropical areas, towering mountain ranges, and low coastlines. Once lush and abundant in wildlife and vegetation, Haiti has suffered severe ecological damage that has wiped out most of its indigenous plant and animal life. Since the arrival of European explorer Christopher Columbus in 1492, Haitians have known virtually nothing but hardship and struggles, yet they have one of the most colorful and lively cultures in the world. Haiti has produced fearless leaders, wonderful artists and writers, and music that is enjoyed worldwide. As the Caribbean's first free republic, Haiti has inspired oppressed people everywhere.

Opposite: **A Haitian driver sits atop his car in a busy Port-au-Prince street.**

Below: **Haiti's markets bustle with energy and activity. This man is selling bread out of a large basket.**

THE FLAG OF HAITI

The Haitian flag traces its roots to 1803, after Haitians won their final victory over French colonial forces. Haitian leader Jean-Jacques Dessalines created it by taking the French red, blue, and white flag, turning it on its side, and removing the white band. The coat of arms and motto were added later. The flag consists of two horizontal bands of blue and red, with a white rectangle in the center that bears the Haitian coat of arms: a palm tree flanked by flags and two cannons. The motto beneath the coat of arms reads *l'union fait la force*, which means "union makes strength."

Geography

Haiti occupies the western third of the island of Hispaniola in the Caribbean Sea. The Atlantic Ocean borders Haiti's northern coast, while the Caribbean Sea lies off the western and southern shores. Haiti shares Hispaniola with the Dominican Republic, which lies on Haiti's eastern border.

Haiti consists of two peninsulas separated by the Golfe de la Gonâve, or Gonâve Gulf. The total land area of the country is 10,641 square miles, (27,560 square kilometers) and includes four important islands: Île de la Gonâve, located in the Gonâve Gulf; Île de la Tortue, or Tortuga Island, situated off Haiti's northern coast; Île-à-Vache, lying south of Haiti's southern shoreline; and Grande Cayemite, which lies off the northern coast of Haiti's southern peninsula.

Above: Waterfalls and lakes are part of Haiti's mountainous countryside.

Mountainous Terrain

More than two-thirds of Haiti is mountainous. Several mountain ranges cross the country, dividing it into three regions: northern, central, and southern. These ranges include the Massif de la Hotte

Below: Haiti has many coves and bays with beautiful beaches.

and the Massif des Montagnes Noires. The highest peak, Pic la Selle, rises 8,793 feet (2,680 meters) in southeastern Haiti.

Only about 20 percent of Haiti is considered arable land. The three major agricultural regions are the Plaine du Nord, the Artibonite River Valley, and the Cul-de-Sac Plain. All three regions are located in Haiti's inland areas.

Above: **An aerial view of northwestern Haiti shows rich, green agricultural fields.**

Rivers and Lakes

Numerous swift rivers flow down from the mountains. The Artibonite, the largest of these rivers, is the only navigable river in Haiti. Beginning in central Haiti, near the border with the Dominican Republic, the Artibonite flows west toward the coast. It meets the Caribbean Sea north of the town of Saint-Marc.

Haiti has both freshwater and saltwater lakes. Haiti's largest lake, Étang Saumâtre, is located in the southeastern part of the country, near the border with the Dominican Republic.

DEFORESTATION IN HAITI

Haiti suffers from extensive deforestation, soil erosion, and inadequate supplies of potable, or drinkable, water. Much of the remaining forests are being cleared for farming.
(A Closer Look, page 46)

Seasons

While the climate in Haiti is mainly tropical, temperature and rainfall vary according to elevation and exposure to the northeast trade winds. Generally speaking, three climatic regions can be defined: the southern region, the central region, and the northern region. The climate is different in each of these regions. The southern region experiences two rainy seasons: from March to early June and from August to October. The central region has one rainy season from April to October, while the northern region's rainy season lasts from September to June.

Average annual rainfall can vary from a high of 144 inches (366 centimeters) on the western tip of the southern peninsula to only 24 inches (61 cm) on the southwestern coast of the country's northern peninsula.

Areas in Haiti that are not exposed to the trade winds, such as the eastern lowlands, tend to be hot and dry. Trade winds cannot reach these areas because they are blocked by high mountains.

The country's capital, Port-au-Prince, which is located at sea level, has an annual average temperature of 80° Fahrenheit (27° Celsius). Temperatures drop slightly as elevation increases, but even at Haiti's highest points temperatures rarely drop below 60° F (16° C).

HURRICANES

Haiti lies in the hurricane belt and is subject to severe storms and flooding from June to October. Haiti was struck by devastating hurricanes in 1963, 1980, 1988, 1994, and 1998. The last major hurricane to hit Haiti, Hurricane Georges in 1998, caused flash floods and mud slides that took the lives of many people. Haitian government officials estimated that over 160,000 people were left homeless as a result of the destruction caused by Hurricane Georges.

Below: Farmers return home with their donkeys after a day's work in the dry southeastern part of Haiti.

Left: Manatees, or sea cows, are endangered marine mammals that live in small numbers in some of Haiti's mangrove swamps.

Plants and Animals

Haiti's once abundant and striking tropical plant and animal life has been significantly reduced due to environmental problems.

Clearing trees for farms and fuel has robbed Haiti of most of its forests, although it still has pine forests at high elevations and mangroves in swamps. Here and there, a lone silk-cotton tree can be seen. These trees are often saved because many Haitians believe they are the habitats of spirits. Many varieties of the palm tree also dot the landscape. These species include the royal palm, which is found on Haiti's flag and coat of arms. In the desertlike lowlands, vegetation consists mainly of cactus and scrub brush.

Plants grown for agricultural purposes include coffee plants and cacao, avocado, citrus, and banana trees. Other crops include rice, corn, sugarcane, sweet potatoes, manioc, and cotton.

Many native animals in Haiti have been hunted to extinction. Some species, however, still survive in places such as Étang Saumâtre, Haiti's largest lake, where manatees, crocodiles, flamingos, and several species of fish thrive.

Preservation efforts have managed to save more than eighty species of birds in the mountain regions, including the endangered peregrine falcon, which winters in Haiti. Small animals of this region include butterflies, snails, frogs, and bats. The desert regions are home to the rhinoceros iguana, a large endangered lizard, as well as other species of lizards and snakes.

Above: The majestic peregrine falcon winters in Haiti's tropical climate.

THE PALM TREE

The palm tree is found everywhere in Haiti, and Haitians make use of nearly every part of the tree and fruit. The palm tree can also be found on the country's flag.

(A Closer Look, page 62)

History

The Arrival of Christopher Columbus

When Christopher Columbus landed on Hispaniola in 1492, the island had already been inhabited for hundreds of years by a group of people called the Taino, or Arawak. The Taino called their land *Ayiti*, or "mountainous." Columbus traded with the natives for gold trinkets. Wishing to find the source of this gold, Spain began to colonize Ayiti. Colonial rule destroyed the Taino. In 1492, hundreds of thousands of Taino lived on Ayiti. By 1550, however, slavery, murder, and diseases against which they had no natural immunities had wiped out their race.

The Spanish finally realized that the new settlement lacked extensive mineral riches. Spain then turned its sights elsewhere in the Caribbean and greatly neglected Ayiti. It was this neglect over the next century and a half that left the island open to invasion from other countries.

THE TAINO

The Taino were living on Hispaniola when Columbus landed there in 1492. They had a well-organized society and had established a flourishing civilization.
(A Closer Look, page 68)

Left: **In a style characteristic of colonial art of the time, this sixteenth-century illustration shows a Taino man and woman as seen by a European artist.**

The French and Saint-Domingue

The French began settling on Île de la Tortue in 1659. Soon, they also began to settle on the northwest corner of Ayiti, and, in 1670, they established a community there called Cap-Français (now Cap-Haïtien). Spain gave France control of the western portion of Hispaniola in 1697. Ayiti was renamed Saint-Domingue, and, by the mid-eighteenth century, France had turned Saint-Domingue into the richest colony in the Americas.

Under French rule, thousands of slaves were brought from Africa to Saint-Domingue to work on plantations. A small group of white people ruled the island. Mulattoes, people of mixed black and white ancestry, could own land, but they could not hold political power. The majority of the population consisted of brutally treated black slaves who had no rights whatsoever.

The French Revolution began in France in 1789 and resulted in widespread political changes in France as well as in French colonies overseas. The government of France ordered the government of Saint-Domingue to allow landowning mulattoes the right to vote. The colonial government refused and faced heated protests from the mulatto landowners. In 1791, slaves in Saint-Domingue revolted against the government. The revolt was ignited during a religious service, when the slaves were encouraged to seek justice for all the years of oppression they had endured under the tyranny of mulatto and French plantation owners.

PIRATES AHOY!

Some of the first French people to settle on the island of Hispaniola were pirates.
(A Closer Look, page 64)

11

Haiti from 1804 to 1934

Initially led by François Toussaint L'Ouverture (c.1743–1803), the rebels fought bitterly. After years of setbacks, violence, numerous casualties, and efforts by France to quell the revolution, the slaves emerged victorious. On January 1, 1804, Haiti proclaimed its independence from France and became the first free black republic in the world. Toussaint did not live to see it.

Jean-Jacques Dessalines (c.1758–1806), another rebel leader, crowned himself emperor of Haiti and imposed a forced labor system, with a newly formed military to keep it in place. However, conflicts between whites, mulattoes, and blacks increased, and Dessalines lost support. In 1806, he was assassinated.

From 1806 to 1915, Haiti had over twenty-two heads of state, most of whom were assassinated, overthrown, or forced to resign. These changes of government were very unstable for the country.

On July 27, 1915, Haitian president Guillaume Sam executed 167 political prisoners. After this violent act, the United States decided to intervene. Within six weeks, U.S. representatives controlled all Haitian customs houses and administrative institutions. For the next 19 years, U.S. marines occupied Haiti, and the U.S. government guided and governed the country.

Above: **Jean-Jacques Dessalines (*left*) and Henri Christophe (*right*) were important heroes of the Haitian revolution.**

FOUNDING FATHERS

The Founding Fathers of Haiti are remembered today for the heroic actions that freed Haiti from French rule.
(A Closer Look, page 52)

The Duvalier Regime (1957–1986)

By 1934, U.S. troops had withdrawn from Haiti, leaving the country with no central government. The Haitian military then became a central force in governing Haiti. The military helped the next Haitian presidents establish their power. In 1957, physician François Duvalier (1907–1971), or "Papa Doc," became president and began an era of dictatorship and rule by force.

Papa Doc replaced all existing government officials with ones of his own choice. In 1964, he declared himself president for life. He formed a police force called the *Tonton Macoutes* (tohntohn mah-KOOT). This police force kept Papa Doc in power by terrorizing the population. An estimated 30,000 Haitians were killed by the Tonton Macoutes during Papa Doc's rule.

Papa Doc's son, Jean-Claude Duvalier (1951–) succeeded him at his death. Jean-Claude, or "Baby Doc," used his position to embezzle money from the treasury. Haitians grew more and more tired of his corruption, and violent street protests broke out in the mid-1980s. In February 1986, Baby Doc fled Haiti for France.

THE DUVALIER DYNASTY

The Duvalier family ruled Haiti for nearly thirty years. They left the country with no money, no working political institutions, and no infrastructure.
(*A Closer Look*, page 48)

Below: Soldiers of the Tonton Macoutes pose during a military parade in the 1960s.

13

Democracy at Last?

From 1986 until 1990, Haiti was ruled by a series of provisional governments. In 1990, Jean-Bertrand Aristide (1953–) was elected president. Within seven months, however, he was overthrown by a military coup and exiled. After much turmoil and more intervention by the United States, Aristide returned in October 1994 and served out his remaining term.

Aristide's prime minister, René Préval (1943–), served as president between 1996 and 2000. In the 2000 elections, Aristide ran for president again and won. His hopes are to focus on much-needed improvements in Haiti's economy and to strengthen the country's central government.

Democracy in Haiti is still fragile. Elections in the 1990s were marked by violence and allegations of voting irregularities. There continue to be reports of torture and brutality. Haiti's infrastructure remains weak, and drug trafficking has corrupted both the judicial system and the police force. The country's most serious social problem is the large economic gap between the impoverished Creole-speaking black majority and the French-speaking mulattoes, who control nearly half of Haiti's wealth despite forming only about one percent of the population.

Left: **Jean-Claude Duvalier officiates at a parade in Port-au-Prince in 1976.**

François Macandal (?–1758)

During the 1700s, groups of runaway slaves known as *marrons* (MAH-ron) banded together in small colonies in the harsh mountain regions of Haiti. These bands would carry out attacks on the French plantation owners. The most famous marron leader was François Macandal, an African born in Guinea. Macandal was reported to be knowledgeable in voodoo practices and skilled in making weapons. In 1751, he led a rebellion that lasted until 1757 and left six thousand people dead. He was captured in 1758 and burned at the stake by the French. He became a legend after his execution. Many Haitians consider Macandal's revolt as the first important sign of dissatisfaction against the French.

Simone Ovide Duvalier (1913–1997)

Simone Ovide Duvalier, or "Mama Doc," was the wife of François Duvalier and mother of Jean-Claude Duvalier, two of Haiti's most infamous leaders. As a young woman, she trained as a nurse's aide and met and married a young doctor named François Duvalier.

Simone Ovide Duvalier

Simone is often regarded as the power behind the rule of both Papa and Baby Doc. Her power increased in 1971, when François died and left the presidency to his son. Baby Doc had little interest in politics and allowed his mother to run the country. When Baby Doc fled Haiti for France in 1986, Simone went with him. She died in France in 1997. Simone was one of the few women in Haiti's stormy history who managed to gain significant political power.

René Garcia Préval (1943–)

Préval was born in Haiti in 1943. As a young man, he spent twelve years in exile with his politically persecuted family.

René Garcia Préval

Upon his return to Haiti in 1975, Préval became highly active in the anti-Duvalier movement. In 1991, he was appointed prime minister. He gained a reputation as a good and efficient administrator and was elected president in 1995. Préval's swearing in as president in 1996 was the first peaceful transfer of power from one democratically elected president to another in all of Haiti's turbulent history.

Government and the Economy

Haiti became an independent republic on January 1, 1804. Since then, many military leaders and dictators have controlled the government. The current constitution, approved in 1987, does call for democratic elections. This constitution was suspended, however, after a coup in June 1988. The constitution was partially reinstated in March 1989. Constitutional rule did not truly begin in Haiti until the latter part of 1994.

Under the constitution, the central governing body consists of three branches of state: the executive, the legislative, and the judicial. The president, who is elected by the people for a five-year term, is the head of the executive branch. The president appoints a prime minister from the majority party in the legislature. The prime minister enforces the laws and, together with the president, is responsible for national defense. The

Below: **The Palais National (National Palace) in Port-au-Prince is a beautiful white building built in the colonial style. It is the residence of the president of Haiti.**

Left: **Military troops march past government buildings in Port-au-Prince. The Palais National can be seen in the background.**

president and prime minister also appoint the members of the various ministries, including commerce and industry, social affairs, finance and economy, and women's affairs. The legislative branch must approve the appointments.

The legislative branch, called parliament, is formed by two groups: the Chamber of Deputies and the Senate. The Chamber of Deputies is a group of elected officials who serve for four-year terms and can be reelected an indefinite number of times. The Senate members are elected for six years and can also be reelected over and over again. The main duty of the legislative branch is to oversee activities of the executive branch and approve new laws handed down by the executive.

The judicial branch is made up of various courts, the highest of which is the Supreme Court, or Cour de Cassation. Its main objective is to carry out the administration of justice throughout the country. Haitian law is based on the Roman civil law system.

Haiti has nine provinces, called departments. They are: the Artibonite, Centre, Grand'Anse, Nord, Nord-Est, Nord-Ouest, Ouest, Sud, and Sud-Est.

Economy

Haiti's economy has been an unpredictable force for many years, and great efforts have been made in recent years to bolster it.

Haiti has few natural resources left, and they are hard to extract from the land. These natural resources include bauxite, copper, calcium carbonate, gold, and marble.

Agriculture is the main economic activity in Haiti despite the problems of deforestation, erosion, and inefficient agricultural techniques. This sector employs about two-thirds of the labor force. Haiti produces considerable amounts of coffee, mangoes, sugarcane, rice, corn, cacao, and sorghum.

Industrial production accounts for the next most important economic activity in Haiti, with some 25 percent of Haitians employed in this sector. Major areas of production include clothes, handicrafts, food and tobacco products, leather goods, furniture, chemicals, steel, cleaning supplies, and toiletries. Banking and financial services, commerce, and tourism employ the remainder of Haiti's active workforce.

Haiti conducts most of its trade with the United States. Haitian exports to the United States include clothes, mangoes,

Below: **Sugarcane is one of Haiti's main agricultural products. These workers are gathering canes that will be shipped to factories. There, the juice is extracted from the canes. Sugar and molasses can then be made from this juice.**

essential oils, toys, sporting goods, and electrical products. Items that are imported from the United States include wheat flour, motor vehicles, soybean oil, machinery, and petroleum.

Above: **Most of Haiti's imports and exports enter and leave the country via ports such as this deep-water port at Cap-Haïtien.**

Transportation and Communications
Haiti's transportation infrastructure is poor. A quarter of Haiti's roads are paved; the rest are dirt or gravel roads. Highways link Port-au-Prince to major cities in the rest of the country. Port-au-Prince has one international airport. There is no passenger rail service or commercial railroad, only a rail line once used to transport sugarcane. Haiti has ports in various cities, including Cap-Haïtien, Gonaïves, Jacmel, Les Cayes, Port-au-Prince, and Saint-Marc. Telecommunication services are concentrated in the capital, with few or no services in most other areas.

Poverty
About 80 percent of Haiti's people fall below the World Bank's absolute poverty level. Its economy has many problems that cannot be solved overnight. Haiti's long line of corrupt and violent government officials are mainly responsible for this state of affairs. Haiti depends greatly on foreign aid and is the poorest country in the Western Hemisphere.

People and Lifestyle

Different Social Classes

Ninety-five percent of Haitians are of African origin; five percent are white or mulatto. Mulattoes and whites make up nearly all of the country's elite. The elite speak mainly French, while the rest of the population tends to speak mainly Creole. It is difficult for a dark-skinned person in Haiti to reach elite status. Throughout Haitian history, distinctions in economic class and social status have been decided by the color of one's skin, the language one speaks, and the work one performs.

The only group in Haiti that could be described as an ethnic minority is a small population of Arabs. Arab traders began arriving from Lebanon and Syria in the late nineteenth century, and some Arabs still remain in Haiti today. Many Haitian-Arabs have adopted French as their preferred language and specialize in trading. They have used their language and business skills as well as their lighter skin to gain entry into Haiti's elite.

LIVELY PORT-AU-PRINCE

Port-au-Prince, Haiti's largest city, is rich in culture and history. It is also a city of contrasts, where the class known as the elite mingles with the so-called lower classes. (*A Closer Look, page 60*)

Below: Haiti's population has a small mulatto minority (*left*); the majority of the people are of African ancestry (*right*).

Left: Haitians value family ties. This woman poses with her infant outside a Port-au-Prince church.

Elite Haitians hold positions in industry, trade, and real estate. Being a member of the elite requires a thorough knowledge of cultural refinements, especially the traditions of the French. The elite live posh, expensive lifestyles that make use of their wealth. The wealthiest Haitians live in gated communities, dine at fine restaurants and night clubs, and visit expensive shopping centers.

The majority of Haiti's poor population, known as the lower classes, live in rural areas. They farm small plots of infertile land that seldom yield enough to feed them. These peasants have little or no access to clean water and have little hope of ever moving up Haiti's social ladder. Most of these farmers either live too far away to send their children to school or else cannot spare their labor on the farms.

A small percentage of Haiti's lower class, about 20 percent, lives in the cities. For the lower class, living conditions in the city are considerably worse than in rural areas. The poor live in overcrowded slums. They are unemployed or earn too little to support themselves. The urban poor do not have access to good health care, proper sanitation, or even safe, affordable drinking water. Despite economic hardships, urban lower-class parents make a concerted effort to keep their children in school, knowing it is their only way to a better life.

HEALTH IN HAITI

Haiti lacks a proper health care system. As a result, many Haitians suffer from illnesses that are preventable.
(A Closer Look, page 58)

A FARMER'S LIFE

Most Haitians work as farmers and lead very difficult lives. Some farming communities have formed cooperatives and associations to help farmers improve their economic situation.
(A Closer Look, page 50)

The Extended Family

Haitians place great importance on family ties. In rural areas, the extended family has traditionally been the main social unit. Until the early part of the twentieth century, the *lakou* (lah-KOOH), or extended family consisting of aunts, uncles, cousins, in-laws, and grandparents, was the principal family group. The lakou was usually named for the head male's lineage and referred to both the family members and the large cluster of houses in which they lived. Members of the lakou worked cooperatively and provided each other with financial and emotional support.

Although the lakou system has declined, many Haitians still live with and support members of their extended family where possible. Sometimes, however, Haitians do not have enough money or space to care for their extended family. Nowadays, Haitians usually rely on their nuclear family rather than on their extended family.

Children

Haitian parents consider children gifts from God. Parents work hard to provide for them, ensure them a good education, and divide inheritances equally. In return, when the children grow up, they care for their aging parents. It is rare in Haiti for children not to care for their parents as their parents grow older.

Left: **These two sisters are dressed in their best clothes for their First Holy Communion ceremony in a church in Port-de-Paix.**

The Role of Men and Women

In general, Haitian men and women share household and financial responsibilities equally. Women assist in farm work by weeding and harvesting. At home, women usually are responsible for child care and daily household tasks. Men do the rest of the farming and help out around the house with heavy chores such as gathering firewood.

Haitian women are very active in the labor force. In Haiti's profitable coffee industry, for example, it is the women who bring the coffee to sell in the markets. Income earned from businesses other than farming does not have to be shared with the husband. As a result, many women have become financially independent.

Marriage

Haiti's lower classes practice a type of common-law marriage known as *plasaj* (plah-SAHJ). It does not entail an official civil ceremony. Plasaj is considered proper and normal among the poor. The elite, however, hold civil or religious marriages in high esteem. The "best" families can trace their legally and officially married ancestors all the way back to the nineteenth century.

Above: **A Haitian trader rides to market to sell her plump chickens.**

WOMEN IN HAITI

Women in Haiti have traditionally played a more active part in the economy than women in most other countries in the region.

(A Closer Look, page 72)

Education

Haiti's first schools were established shortly after independence. Although education is compulsory in Haiti, only about 73 percent of all children below the age of twelve actually attend school. About 63 percent of these children complete their primary education. Only about 53 percent of Haitian adults are literate.

Most children live too far from the closest school to make regular attendance possible. Classes are taught mainly in French, while the majority of Haitians speak only Creole. Families also cannot afford the cost of school uniforms and supplies. Teachers are often poorly trained and badly paid.

Those who do attend school, however, study in a system modeled after the French education system. Literature and the humanities are the main emphases, with rural schools specializing in vocational education and agricultural studies.

The Reforms of 1978

In 1978, the education system was reformed to make education more accessible and relevant to the poor. These reforms instituted

Below: **Young children attend class in a school in Port-au-Prince.**

Left: Young adults pay attention to a carpentry lesson in a vocational college in Port-au-Prince.

ten years of primary education, consisting of four years of preparatory classes, three years of elementary classes, and three years of intermediate classes. Students then take exams to enter public or private secondary schools for three more years.

The 1978 reforms made Haitian Creole the language of instruction in the preparatory classes. This law has been difficult to implement because some teachers refuse to teach in Creole. They consider the language inferior to French.

Higher Education

The State University of Haiti was established in 1944. It offers courses in medicine, law, business, agricultural studies, social sciences, architecture, and engineering. University Quisqueya opened in 1988 and offers many fields of study, including nursing and teaching. Other institutions of higher learning include the École Supérieure d'Infotronique d'Haïti, which specializes in information technology studies.

Religion

Eighty percent of Haitians are Roman Catholics, while 16 percent belong to various Protestant churches, including Pentecostal, Baptist, and Adventist churches. About 4 percent of Haitians belong to other religions or none at all. Voodoo may be considered the national religion. Most Haitians, including Catholics and Protestants, also practice at least some aspect of voodoo.

Popular misconceptions about voodoo have created a negative stereotype about both rituals and believers. Many people believe voodoo is a cult of sorcerers who practice black magic, when, in reality, the majority of voodoo is based on family spirits who help and protect. Voodoo has its roots in African beliefs. When Africans of various tribes were brought to Haiti as slaves, they brought with them beliefs in different spirits. In time, the various different African beliefs and rituals combined to form voodoo.

While Haitian voodoo lacks a fixed theology and organized hierarchy, it still has its own rituals, ceremonies, and symbols. Haitian voodoo believers do not find voodoo practices at odds with Christian religion. Many Roman Catholic and Protestant symbols and prayers have been blended with voodoo to create a unique and typically Haitian religion.

VODUN RELIGION

Vodun (voh-DAHN), more popularly known as voodoo, is widely practiced in Haiti.
(A Closer Look, page 70)

Left: Nativity scenes such as this one are common during Christmastime in Haiti.

Christianity in Haiti

Roman Catholicism began to gain popularity in Haiti in the late 1800s, when white plantation owners passed the religion on to their slaves. Many slaves were forced to accept their masters' wishes, but the slaves could not face spiritual as well as bodily enslavement. Their need to keep some piece of their own identity led to the mixing of their native voodoo beliefs with Catholicism. While Roman Catholic clergy are opposed to voodoo, they are considerably more tolerant than Protestant church leaders.

Protestantism has existed in Haiti since the earliest days of the republic. Missionaries established churches and missions throughout Haiti. Conversion to Protestantism began in earnest in the 1950s, and the number of believers has grown since then. Most Protestant doctrines strongly object to voodoo and consider it evil and demonic. Thus, unlike Haitian Catholics, Haitian Protestants cannot easily retain parts of voodoo religion. Haiti's Protestants, however, still find it hard to escape the influence of voodoo, as the religion pervades much of everyday Haitian life.

Above: Haitians perform a voodoo ceremony. Many Haitians practice some form of voodoo even though they are also Roman Catholic or Protestant Christians.

Language and Literature

Language and Class

The two official languages of Haiti are French and Haitian Creole. All Haitians speak Haitian Creole, but only 10 percent of the population speaks French as well. French is the language of the government and many Haitian schools, however, and therefore retains its status as a national language.

French settlers brought their language to Haiti. Only the settlers and a few mulatto free men spoke French, and its use became a tool to distinguish between social classes. Haitian Creole was considered the everyday language of the people, and French was the language for formal situations. In recent years, there have been efforts to use Haitian Creole in more formal business and official situations. In business and among young people, the use of English is also growing.

Haitian Creole

Even though Haitian Creole was most likely based on French, it is entirely different, with more similarities to the many African dialects of the slaves. Some linguists believe that Haitian Creole

CITY OF POETS

The town of Jérémie in southwestern Haiti is home to many writers and artists.
(A Closer Look, page 44)

Below: **An election poster displays words in Haitian Creole.**

28

originated when the French slave masters needed a way to communicate with their slaves, and the slaves with each other.

The Oral Tradition

Haitian literature began with storytelling. In the past, Haiti's largely illiterate population passed on their histories and myths through storytelling. Haiti's rich oral tradition still exists today, and storytelling is considered a performance art. The storyteller uses a different voice for each character and often weaves songs and riddles into the story.

Literature

Haiti has produced famous writers, poets, and essayists. Most Haitian literature is in French. Writers have only recently begun to use Creole. *Dézafi,* the first full-length novel written entirely in Creole, was written by Franck Étienne and published in 1975.

In general, Haiti has two main types of literature: one that embraces the pains and sufferings of the everyday life of Haitian people, and one that focuses on Haitian exploits, history, shames, and defeats.

Haitian author Edwidge Danticat was born and raised in Haiti. She has gained critical acclaim for her writing. Her 1994 novel *Breath, Eyes, Memory* tells the story of four Haitian women overcoming poverty and oppression.

HAITI'S ORAL TRADITIONS

Haitians enjoy telling jokes, riddles, proverbs, and folktales. These oral traditions help Haitians relax and take their minds off the difficult conditions in which they live.

(A Closer Look, page 56)

Arts

Haiti's unique culture and rich traditions are reflected in
its arts. Much of life for Haitians is harsh and difficult. By
contrast, Haitian art is colorful and vibrant. The enthusiasm
and imagination of Haitian artists are reflected in different
forms of art. Even the poorest Haitians express themselves
through murals painted on slum walls or on the sides of a
tap-tap (tup-TUP), a private bus used for public transportation.

Haitian Art Discovered

For many years, international art critics and the Haitian elite
overlooked the popular artistic expressions in Haiti. In the 1940s,
Haitian art received international attention and rapidly gained
popularity. American watercolorist DeWitt Peters is often credited

Below: **Haitian
paintings are colorful
and deeply symbolic.**

with making Haitian paintings famous abroad. Peters established the Centre d'Art in 1944, which was a key factor in the discovery and marketing of Haitian art. Critics began praising Haitian self-taught artists and their painting style.

Above: **Handicrafts are a thriving industry in Haiti. This girl in Port-de-Paix browses through a collection of elegant straw hats.**

Evolving Styles

Primitivism is the oldest and most popular style of painting. Artists of the primitive style were self-taught artists who gained their recognition in the 1940s. Although they lacked formal training, their work was still meaningful and aesthetically pleasing. Art historians date this style to 1940, even though Haitian farmers had been painting in this style since the 1800s.

During the 1960s and 1970s, the repressive atmosphere of the Duvalier regime produced more technically perfect and formal paintings that lacked much of the passion and fire of the primitive style. In recent years, with more opportunities for formal art studies, many Haitian painters have combined the liveliness of the primitive style with formal techniques to make truly beautiful and collectible Haitian art. Collecting Haitian art does not have to be expensive. Each day at Haitian markets, hundreds of beautiful paintings are for sale at very affordable prices.

Above: A couple holds up a Haitian prayer flag. Prayer flags are colorful pieces of cloth embroidered with elaborate patterns and shiny sequins. They are used in voodoo ceremonies and have become works of art in their own right.

Haitian Music

A famous Haitian dance and musical style is merengue, a ballroom dance of Dominican and Haitian origin. This style developed during the nineteenth century, when Haitian musicians began combining European classical music and African drumming and dancing.

Other modern musical styles include *compas* (KOM-pah) and *mizik rasin* (mee-ZIHK rah-SEEN), or roots music. Compas music is very popular and combines jazz, merengue, and rock 'n' roll with voodoo drum beats. This type of music appeals largely to younger Haitians and is often played at parties and dance clubs. Roots music developed in the 1980s when Haitian music and voodoo music experienced a revival of interest. Roots music was a way to bring Haitian culture to a new generation of Haitians, as well as to the world. The band Boukman Eksperyans is a famous band that plays roots music.

Haitian voodoo ceremonies feature much music, singing, and dancing. Followers use rattles, conch shells, drums, and bamboo flutes to produce lively rhythms and tunes.

SINGING SENSATIONS

Music is an important part of Haitian culture, and the country has produced many singers who have become internationally famous.
(*A Closer Look*, page 66)

Haitian Architecture

Haiti has a number of famous buildings that attract visitors. Several Roman Catholic cathedrals dot the country's various cities. The Cathédrale de la Ste Trinité in Port-au-Prince features beautiful murals. The Citadelle LaFerrière and the Palais de Sans Souci are the two most noteworthy buildings in Haiti. They were built in the early nineteenth century by Henri Christophe (1767–1820), who declared himself emperor of Haiti in 1811. The restored citadel and the Sans Souci ruins are located south of Cap-Haïtien.

Sculptures and Handicrafts

Many Haitians sculpt in metals such as iron or aluminum and sell their creations in open-air markets. Oil drum art, for example, is created from the lid of an oil drum. The lid is hammered, cut, and soldered into a lovely sculpture. Carnival masks and baskets are also important pieces of Haitian art. They once were considered simple handicrafts, but a recent craze for Haitian art has turned handicrafts into recognized and important forms of artistic expressions highly sought after by collectors.

GRANDIOSE MONUMENTS

Haiti has a number of historic buildings that have been constructed on a very large scale.
(A Closer Look, page 54)

Below: **The streets of Port-au-Prince and other Haitian cities are lined with old buildings that are brightly painted. This building houses government offices in Haiti's capital city.**

Leisure and Festivals

Leisure Activities in Haiti

Entertainment in Haiti is usually family oriented and low cost. In terms of organized entertainment venues, Haiti is limited. Those with extra money to spend can go to a dance club or see a floor show at various hotels, but these people are few and far between. Many theaters put on performances, both in French as well as in Creole. Port-au-Prince also has a number of cinemas that show the latest French and U.S. films, all dubbed in French.

Music and Dance

The Haitian people's passion for music and dance plays a large role in leisure activities. Nearly every Saturday evening, families and friends gather in their homes to eat, drink, dance, and tell stories. This gathering is referred to as a *bamboche* (bum-BAWSH). At a bamboche, the events of the week are discussed and jokes and riddles exchanged. The evenings usually end with a story or two.

Below: Beautiful Haitian beaches like this one are usually reserved for tourists. Others, however, are open to Haitians, and many pass their leisure time there.

Haitian Games

Haitians also enjoy games, especially board and card games. Chess sets, carved from available woods, are popular, as are checkers, tic-tac-toe, and dominoes. Betting is also a common form of entertainment, and many people bet weekly on the local street-corner lottery called *borlette* (bore-LET). It is said that players rely on dreams to decide what lottery numbers to choose.

Religious Activities

Haitians spend a lot of their leisure time participating in religious activities. Haiti has a very religious culture, and masses in Catholic churches are well attended even on weekdays. Haitian believers are likely to supplement regular masses with less frequent trips to the local voodoo temple. Haitians may visit the temple less often because most voodoo ceremonies require food or some other material sacrifice, while masses require nothing but a willing spirit. For some Haitians, religious activities help them unload their daily burdens and temporarily forget their problems.

Above: **Haitians meet at markets not only to buy and sell goods, but also to exchange information and the latest gossip.**

Cockfighting

One of the most popular national pastimes is holding a cockfight. It is the sport of choice for the Haitian peasantry. Cockfights take place every Sunday in almost every village and neighborhood across the country. The birds all have names, and the sport is practiced at a local pit, or *gagé* (GAH-zhay). The spectators and owners gather around the pit to make comments on the fight and offer advice. Betting is common at these events, and a lot of money changes hands. A successful trainer can become a powerful figure in the community.

Cockfights are sometimes bloody and continue until one of the birds tires. Before the fight begins, the birds are paraded around the pit along with their owners. A fight can sometimes take as long as half an hour.

The cockfight is often seen as representing the Haitians' tireless fight for freedom. The symbolism of the cockfight is not lost on politicians. To identify with common Haitians, President Aristide used the symbol of a fighting cock during his election campaigns.

Below: **Cockfighting is an extremely popular sport in Haiti.**

Left: **Chris Armas (*right*), of the U.S. national soccer team, and Michel Gabriel (*left*), of Haiti, battle for the ball during a soccer game in Miami, Florida, in 2000.**

Soccer

Soccer, or football as it is called in Haiti, is a well-loved sport. Huge crowds are drawn to soccer matches at the Sylvio Cator Stadium in Port-au-Prince. This well-built facility is a mark of the sport's importance in Haiti, a country that has little money to spare for recreational and sporting activities. In 1974, Haiti became only the second Caribbean nation to qualify for the World Cup Competition.

Soccer is not just for professionals. Haitians of all ages play soccer throughout the country on dirt roads and fields. Soccer is also a sport that is enjoyed by both the elite and the lower classes.

Joe Gaetjens and Emmanuel Sanon are two of Haiti's professional soccer players. Many young Haitian soccer players aspire to be as famous as these sportsmen.

The Christmas Season

The Christmas season in Haiti lasts for nearly a month. It begins around the middle of December, with Haitians choosing a Christmas tree to decorate. Pine trees in Haiti are too rare to be chopped down entirely every year, so families will cut branches from a huge, older pine and use them as a tree. The pine tree continues to grow, providing a steady supply of branches. Nativity scenes are also highly popular Christmas decorations.

During the Christmas season, children set off a special type of firework called *klorat* (CLAW-raht). The Duvalier regime banned these fireworks for many years, but they have recently made a comeback. On Christmas Eve, families attend a midnight mass, followed by a late informal supper, which usually consists of rice and beans. Christmas Day is spent opening gifts, and the next few weeks are spent sharing gifts with friends and visitors.

The Christmas season continues with two patriotic holidays. On January 1, Haitians celebrate Independence Day, and on January 2, they mark Ancestors' Day. The Christmas season officially ends on the first Sunday after Ancestors' Day. This

Below: **Haitians on horseback set out for a famous Haitian town, Saut d'Eau, which is the site of an annual pilgrimage. Haitians believe the town's waterfalls can cure illnesses.**

day is called King's Day. Families gather together once again to enjoy a meal of barbecued goat or pork and fried plantains. Games are played and songs sung as the Christmas trees and nativity scenes are taken down and put away for next year.

Carnival, Lent, and Easter

Carnival, which is celebrated for several days before Ash Wednesday, falls either in February or March. This is a joyful celebration of Haitian arts and culture, with nonstop music, colorful costumes and masks, floats and pageants, and frenzied dancing and processions.

Lent begins on Ash Wednesday and ends forty days later with Easter. Roman Catholic practices are mixed with voodoo ritual during the celebration of these holidays, and musical bands called *ra-ra* (RAH-rah) bands play frequently during this time.

Easter Sunday is the high point of ra-ra band celebrations. The bands move from the voodoo temples through the streets of Haiti in colorful processions. Members wear outlandish clothing and are accompanied by music and heavy drumming.

Above: **Carnival in Haiti is a vibrant and colorful celebration. People dress up in gaudy costumes, and music plays nonstop throughout the day and night.**

OTHER HOLIDAYS

Haitians celebrate a number of patriotic and historical holidays. These holidays include the anniversary of Dessalines's death on October 17, the anniversary of the victory over Napoleon at Vertières on November 18, and the anniversary of Columbus's arrival on December 5.

Food

Haitian cuisine is a combination of the culinary traditions of the countries historically associated with Haiti. These nations include a variety of African nations as well as France, Spain, and the United States. Haitian food is similar to other Caribbean food, except that it is a bit more peppery. Staple Haitian dishes include *riz djon-djon* (ree JON-JON), or rice cooked with small black mushrooms, and *riz pois collés* (ree pwah KUHL-lay), or rice and red beans.

Seafood

Haiti's access to the sea and the country's many rivers mean that fish and other seafood are common foods. Both fresh and saltwater fish are eaten boiled or fried. A particularly delicious dish is *lambi* (LOM-bee), which is fresh conch in a savory garlic sauce. Also popular are lobster and a main dish that has crab and eggplant as its main ingredients.

Meat

Haitians living in inland areas enjoy eating meat, including pork, chicken, and goat. Haitians also like to eat beef, but the

Left: **Millet grows in Haiti and is sometimes eaten crushed and mixed with water.**

Left: **Plantains, which look similar to bananas, are a common sight in Haiti. Haitians eat these fruits fried, boiled, steamed, or roasted.**

wet weather and lack of flat grazing land make cattle hard to raise. *Griot* (GREE-yoh) is a dish that is particularly popular in rural areas. It is made with either pork or mutton. The meat is first boiled, then fried, and is usually served with a very spicy sauce called *ti-malice* (tee-MAH-liss). Ti-malice is often used to season many savory dishes. Popular poultry dishes include chicken with peas and chicken in sauce.

Other Types of Dishes

Haiti's varied climate produces a large variety of fruits and other ingredients that are used to make typical Haitian dishes. Plantains are plentiful and can be fried and served as either a dessert or a side dish. The farms of Haiti also yield sweet potatoes, coconuts, and grapes, the three main ingredients in *pain patate* (pahn pah-TAHT), a delicious Haitian dessert cake.

Soups are not served frequently due to Haiti's warm climate, but pumpkin soup is a traditional holiday dish.

A CLOSER LOOK AT HAITI

While it is true that Haiti's history is filled with violence, including slavery, military coups, public protests, and dictatorial regimes, the country also has had some triumphs. Haiti was the world's first republic led by a person of African descent. The country threw off slavery through the dedication of heroes such as François Toussaint L'Ouverture and Jean-Jacques Dessalines. Haitian women are also an example to women in other developing countries for the way they have been able to achieve some measure of financial independence.

Opposite: **Young Haitians eat ice cream outside a colorful Cap-Haïtien building.**

Haiti also has much to offer to tourists. The Citadelle LaFerrière and the Palais de Sans Souci are considered some of the finest examples of large-scale Caribbean architecture. Port-au-Prince is a colorful city, where music can be heard on the streets and people are warm and friendly. Jérémie, by comparison, is tranquil, relaxed, and home to some of Haiti's finest writers.

At the start of the twenty-first century, there is hope that some of Haiti's infrastructure, including education, health care, and public services, can be improved and that Haitians will soon be able to enjoy the happiness and prosperity they justly deserve.

Above: **A Haitian man stands before his outdoor arts and crafts display in Port-au-Prince. Many streets in Haitian towns and cities are lined with stalls selling handmade crafts and other items.**

City of Poets

The port of Jérémie is located on the southwest coast of Haiti. It is home to about 45,000 people. Over the years, Jérémie has come to be known as the home of famous writers and artists.

An Idyllic Setting

Jérémie is situated in a relatively remote part of Haiti. It is described by many as a paradise, offering spectacular views of steep mountains and inviting coastlines. Azure waters lap at sandy beaches that are lush with tropical plants, such as banana plants, bougainvillea, coconut palms, and breadfruit trees.

Jérémie's inhabitants are poor. Most of them can only afford to travel on mules. Moreover, roads are in such bad condition that traveling by car is nearly impossible.

Local women bring their laundry to the banks of nearby rivers that empty into the sea. As they do their laundry, they sing songs and their children play on bamboo rafts. Jérémie is a sleepy city, seemingly untouched by time.

Trouble in Paradise

Jérémie is not without its hardships, however. There is little clean drinking water. As a result, typhoid, a disease caused by drinking

Below: **An early eighteenth-century drawing shows the waters off Jérémie.**

Left: **An impressive cathedral dominates Jérémie's vibrant and colorful waterfront.**

contaminated water, is endemic throughout the region. While Jérémie is seldom troubled by the unrest that sometimes affects other parts of Haiti, the city is not immune to political strife. In 1964, Duvalier's Tonton Macoutes massacred hundreds of Jérémie's residents. The survivors were helpless to do anything except bury the dead and move on.

The Writer's Haven

Perhaps it is this unique blend of tranquility and harsh poverty, illness, and violence that makes Jérémie such a haven for writers. Writers and artists from Jérémie include composer Othello Bayard, writer Lilas Desquiron, artist Jacques Saint-Surin, and playwright Syto Cave.

Many books published in Haiti are written by authors living in Jérémie. Even local men and women who hold other full-time jobs take the time to write. The city has many Catholic priests and bishops who teach people how to read and write. For Jérémie, literature is a passion that has made the city famous.

Deforestation in Haiti

The term deforestation refers to the destruction of forests. It occurs where land is permanently converted from forest to non-forest use. Haiti suffers from deforestation; only about 2 percent of Haiti's original forests remain.

Deforestation, Rainfall, and Erosion

Deforestation causes many problems that can combine in a chain reaction to damage the environment. Forests serve to control the climate, especially rainfall. Scientists today believe that if Haiti continues to suffer deforestation at the current rate, the country will soon have to import water.

When trees are removed from the land, soil erosion occurs. Nutrients in the soil drain away, leaving behind bare and barren land. Desertification then occurs. Desertification is another one of Haiti's pressing environmental concerns.

Deforestation and the Need for Fuel

Haitians cut down trees to provide wood for charcoal. Charcoal is the main source of energy in Haiti. Charcoal is cheap, and usually even the poorest people can afford a charcoal-burning stove.

Below: **Haiti suffers from deforestation and has lost practically all of its forest cover. Deforestation has led to soil erosion that leaves many hills barren.**

Haiti's cities consume huge amounts of charcoal and contribute to the felling of millions of trees each year. The charcoal industry is highly lucrative for rich investors, and it also provides jobs for many of Haiti's poor. In the end, however, Haiti's charcoal industry will die out as a result of complete deforestation. The industry's fall will adversely affect the majority of the Haitian population, which is totally dependent on coal.

Above: **This young Haitian works at a plant nursery on the outskirts of Cap-Haïtien. The seedlings grown here will be used for reforestation.**

Possible Solutions

Steps are now being taken to decrease the rate of deforestation in Haiti. Alternative sources of energy, such as natural gas and solar power, are being considered. One option already being tried is solar cooking, which cooks food using only the power of the sun. Solar cooking requires special ovens, longer cooking times, outdoor cooking, and training in new cooking techniques. Cooking cannot be done on cloudy days or at night. Despite these problems, many people believe solar cooking can help stem deforestation in Haiti.

The Duvalier Dynasty

The Doctor-President

François Duvalier started out his professional career as a doctor. He worked in various hospitals and even worked for the U.S. Army in Haiti. He was often called "Papa Doc," a name he loved and used frequently during his rule. He was elected president in 1957. In 1961, he replaced Haitian government officials with his followers and, in 1964, declared himself president for life.

Papa Doc reorganized the military in order to weaken its power. He created two new armed branches — the Presidential Guard and the Volunteers for National Security. The Presidential Guard was responsible for protecting Papa Doc's life and maintaining his power. The Volunteers for National Security was a rural militia group that patrolled the country, watching for and quelling any opposition to the Duvalier regime. More popularly called the Tonton Macoutes, this militia group terrorized the Haitian people and executed an estimated 30,000 Haitians during Duvalier's reign.

Corrupt But Respected

Papa Doc appropriated foreign aid for himself, used treasury money for personal purposes, made up his own rules and laws, and appointed his family and friends to important government jobs. He survived several foreign and domestic challenges

Left: **François Duvalier (*center*) poses with his wife, Simone, (*left*) and their daughter Marie-Denise Dominique (*right*) in a photograph taken shortly before his death in 1971.**

Left: **The Duvalier family and members of the Haitian elite observe a ceremony during Haiti's Independence Day celebration in 1976.**

throughout his term that earned him the respect of many. He also knew the mind of the common people from his experiences as a doctor and played upon their responses to his paternalistic side and the rumors that he was an experienced voodoo sorcerer. Thus, his power remained firmly entrenched at his death in 1971 and passed easily to his only son, Jean-Claude Duvalier.

Baby Doc and the End of the Duvaliers

Jean-Claude Duvalier, or Baby Doc, was only 19 when he took over his father's position. He was uninterested in politics and allowed his mother, Simone Duvalier, to run the government for several years while he misappropriated funds and squandered them. However, his corruption finally came under fire when health epidemics severely crippled Haiti's struggling economy. The public was outraged when Jean-Claude spent over U.S. $3 million on his wedding in 1980.

Pope John Paul II visited Haiti in 1983. Observing the sorry state of the economy and the extreme poverty of the people, the Pope declared, "Something must change here." The people clearly agreed and two years later, revolts and riots began.

Baby Doc tried to appease the people by lowering the cost of food and reshuffling the cabinet, but the rioting and violence increased. The United States became concerned and urged Baby Doc to leave the country. Jean-Claude Duvalier finally fled Haiti for France in 1986, bringing an end to the Duvalier dynasty. Haiti is still suffering the long-term effects of the corrupt regime.

A Farmer's Life

About two-thirds of Haiti's workforce are farmers living and working in the countryside. Haitian farmers work hard to farm the available land. Haiti has a diminishing amount of arable land, and many fields are planted on slopes so steep that farmers must use ropes to secure themselves as they work.

Haitian farmers usually live with their extended families. Their homes are made from common building materials such as palm trunks and branches, aluminum sheets, and cardboard. The diet of farming families is limited to what they can grow.

Difficult Conditions

Most rural areas are undeveloped and lack an infrastructure of any kind. The few established roads are mostly dirt and gravel and are often in poor shape. The lack of roads isolates many farmers. New construction projects are rare because the transportation of supplies is costly. Even news of events

Below: **A father and his two sons water their fields by hand.**

Above: **Peaceful rural settings such as these belie the hard life farmers lead in Haiti.**

happening elsewhere in Haiti and the world takes some time before it reaches Haiti's isolated farming communities.

Farmers have limited access to clean drinking water, which makes it difficult to maintain the health of people and livestock. To compound this problem, there are few medical facilities available to Haitian peasants. Most farming families rely on herbal and folk remedies, and the ill are cared for at home. In spite of this poor infrastructure, farmers must still pay taxes, and they receive no aid from the government.

Hope for a Better Future

Despite their difficult circumstances, Haitian farmers still enjoy life. They often sing as they work, and they gather regularly in small churches to give thanks for what they have. Some farming communities band together to create peasant associations that aim to improve the lives of farmers. One such group in southern Haiti, the Peasant Association of Fondwa, was formed in 1988 and has successfully provided the village of Fondwa and several neighboring communities with many amenities, including clean water, a health clinic, and a primary and secondary school.

Grandiose Monuments

Citadelle LaFerrière

Above the plains of northeastern Haiti, perched atop a mountain called Bonnet-à-l'Evêque, sits the Citadelle LaFerrière, one of Haiti's most imposing buildings.

King Henri Christophe began constructing the Citadelle in the early 1800s. He used forced labor to build his fortress, and many thousands of workers lost their lives building the Citadelle. The Citadelle was built entirely from stone and held together by a mortar made of limestone, molasses, and cow's blood. The construction was completed in 1820, and the fortress could hold enough supplies for the royal family and five thousand soldiers for a year.

Christophe built the Citadelle in anticipation of another invasion by France, which had just relinquished control of Haiti. The Citadelle would have been able to house Christophe, his family, and 5,000 soldiers for up to a year while they fought off the French. The feared invasion never came, however.

Below: **An aerial view of Citadelle LaFerrière shows just how much this magnificent structure dominates the surrounding Haitian countryside.**

Christophe died in 1820. The fortress was abandoned shortly thereafter and stood empty for over a century. Recent renovations have turned it into a popular tourist spot. The Citadelle is listed by the United Nations as a cultural treasure, along with such buildings as the Acropolis in Athens, Greece, and the pyramids of Giza in Egypt.

Above: **The ruins of the Palais de Sans Souci attract visitors from all over the world.**

The Palais de Sans Souci

The Palais de Sans Souci was yet another important building constructed by Henri Christophe. The palace was built in the early 1800s near the town of Milot, 12.4 miles (20 kilometers) south of Cap-Haïtien. In fact, the palace was constructed close to the base of the mountain on which stood the Citadelle LaFerrière.

The palace housed both the royal residence as well as the administrative offices of Christophe's government. Palais de Sans Souci was built to rival the Palace of Versailles in France and was opulently furnished. The palace was abandoned in the 1820s after Christophe's death, but its imposing ruins stand as a witness to the early post-independence years of Haiti's history.

Haiti's Oral Traditions

Haitians pass down their knowledge through proverbs, jokes, riddles, and folktales. These may be told around a dinner table or an evening fire, on trips and visits, or while working on different tasks throughout the day. These oral traditions are used to pass on traditional wisdom and to make difficult lives more bearable.

Proverbs

Haitians, especially rural Haitians, routinely use proverbs in everyday conversations to defend their ideas. There are hundreds of proverbs, each relating to different aspects of

Left: **A popular Haitian proverb teaches that "the donkey sweats so the horse can be decorated with lace." This saying means that lower-class Haitians work very hard so that wealthy Haitians can live very comfortably.**

Left: While working or doing chores, Haitians of all ages enjoy telling jokes and riddles or singing their favorite songs.

Haitian life. Some proverbs are practical, and others are political. One popular proverb, "Uproot the manioc, and clear the land," advocated the overthrow of the Duvalier regime.

Jokes and Folktales

Conversations are not all serious. An example of a Haitian joke would be the following: A man moved from Port-au-Prince to Les Cayes. He was nervous about living there, so he asked a fellow in a bar how he liked living in Les Cayes. "Oh, it's a great place," said the man. "When I came here, I couldn't utter a single word. I had no hair, no job, and no food. They gave me a bed and food and helped me out. Now, as you can see, I am strong and well, and I have a good job." The other man was impressed and said, "Wow! When did you come here?" "Oh," replied the man from Les Cayes, "I was born here."

Folktales are longer, but they also incorporate the same cleverness and humor that is found in Haitian jokes and riddles. Haiti's oral tradition is rich in imagination and traditional wisdom, and it forms an indispensable part of Haitian culture.

HAITIAN RIDDLES

The person who has a riddle to tell says, "*Tim tim* (teem TEEM)." Those who wish to hear it reply, "*Bwa seche* (BWAH sash)." The riddle is then told. The listeners give the answer to the riddle if they know it. If they do not, they say "Bwa seche" again. This phrase means "dry wood" and indicates that the listeners are not clever enough to answer the riddle. An example of a Haitian riddle is as follows: "How many coconuts can you put into an empty sack?" "Only one. After that, the sack is not empty."

Health in Haiti

Haiti's people are vibrant, passionate, and full of life, but the country has a very poorly developed health care system. This, coupled with Haiti's extreme poverty, has resulted in low life expectancy rates: 51 years for a Haitian woman and just 48 years for a Haitian man.

Haiti's Health Problems

Many factors contribute to the poor health of Haiti's population. Water supply and basic sanitation are severely limited throughout the country. Fewer than half of the Haitians living in rural areas have access to clean water. The figure is even lower for city dwellers. Ground water in Haiti is also polluted because of the lack of sewage disposal systems. With no proper sewage disposal system, people dispose of their sewage in any way they can.

Haiti's cultural traditions can sometimes encourage unsafe practices. Some Haitians observe dangerous religious practices, such as administering purgatives to newborns or feeding them solid foods.

Medical facilities are limited and expensive in Haiti, and trained doctors and nurses are few in number. Many people must seek spiritual healers to cure illnesses.

Below: **A billboard in Gonaïves encourages women to vaccinate their children against childhood illnesses.**

58

Left: **Haiti has one of the highest rates of infant mortality in the world. The Haitian health ministry and several international humanitarian groups are working hard to reduce the number of infant deaths in the country.**

The lack of proper health care leaves Haiti's children particularly vulnerable. About three in twenty children die before the age of five. The leading causes of child mortality include diarrhea and typhoid, which are caused by drinking contaminated water; malnutrition, caused by a poor diet; and pneumonia, which can be caused by poor living conditions.

Common Illnesses

Malaria, typhoid, and tuberculosis are three major diseases in Haiti. AIDS, or Acquired Immune Deficiency Syndrome, is also on the rise. Figures for 1999 show that about 5 percent of Haitians are living with the human immunodeficiency virus (HIV) that causes AIDS. Vaccinations and good health care practices could prevent the spread of many diseases.

Health Care Reforms

In 1996, the Ministry of Health introduced a health policy that recognizes the government's obligation to guarantee access to health care for all Haitians. The aims of the policy include providing basic health care and vaccinations at low cost to the public, preventing and controlling the spread of communicable diseases, and upgrading hospitals and clinics.

Lively Port-au-Prince

Haiti's capital city, Port-au-Prince, is located in southwestern Haiti, overlooking the Golfe de la Gonâve. The population of the city was estimated at over two million in 1999. The French founded the port in 1749 and later made it the capital of Saint-Domingue, the colonial name for Haiti. Port-au-Prince retained its status as the capital city when Haiti became independent in 1804.

Today, Port-au-Prince also serves as the country's main port, exporting mainly coffee and sugar. Tourism is an essential part of the city's economy.

City of Contrasts

Port-au-Prince's tall buildings provide places of employment for the country's elite, a large percentage of which resides in the city. Expensive shops and restaurants in the city serve the needs of the elite. Many of their fine homes are located on the hills overlooking the city.

Alongside this wealth and beauty lie pollution, industry, and poverty. Large food-processing plants, as well as soap, textile, and

Below: **Colorful tap-tap buses wait for customers outside the famous Iron Market in Port-au-Prince.**

cement factories line the waterfront. Most streets are crowded with traffic. Beggars and homeless people line the sidewalks. Slums dot much of the city. Cité Soleil, a slum in Port-au-Prince, has been rated one of the worst in the world. The urban poor crowd the streets every day selling items such as ice or sugarcane. Open-air markets fill the streets, and the sellers will accept low payment just so they can make a sale.

Above: **A woman sells her wares along a busy Port-au-Prince street.**

A Cultural City

Port-au-Prince is home to a number of notable cultural landmarks. Le Musée d'Art Haïtien and the Musée du Panthéon Nationale are popular with art lovers. The famous Sainte Trinité Episcopalian Cathedral features breathtaking murals; sculptures done in ceramic, brick, iron, and stone; and an impressive organ and choir. The Palais National and the Notre Dame Catholic Cathedral also attract many tourists. Port-au-Prince is also home to two universities, the State University of Haiti and the University Quisqueya, as well as the Librairie La Pléiade.

The Palm Tree

Palms of various species, including the cherry palm and the royal palm, grow throughout Haiti, and Haitians make excellent use of these versatile trees. The palm tree also is featured on Haiti's flag and coat of arms. Its placement there is perhaps symbolic of the importance of the palm tree in the everyday lives of Haitians.

PALM FIBERS

Palm fibers are an important product of the palm tree. They can be obtained from various parts of the palm, depending on the species, and are used to make ropes, mats, brushes, brooms, carpets, filling for mattresses, and nets. Nets and ropes made of palm fibers are especially good for use at sea, since they are resistant to seawater and bacteria and will not sink.

BUILDINGS AND FURNITURE

Palm trees are useful in the construction of both houses and furniture. Wood for the main and supporting posts of a house can come from the trees' trunks. Flooring material can also be made from the trunks. Palm leaves can make sturdy thatched roofs or partitions for walls. Such housing is perfect in Haiti's tropical climate, and palm materials are cheap and easily available.

Left: Tall palm trees line an intersection in Port-au-Prince.

Left: **A horse carries bunches of palm fruit across a stream in the countryside around Cap-Haïtien.**

Edible Parts of the Palm

Some palm trees produce edible sap. The sap of the cherry palm, for example, is sweet and creamy. It can be fermented and made into wine or crystallized and used as a sweetener. The seeds of many palms make excellent snacks and can also yield oil. Once the oil is extracted, the seeds can still be used as a healthy and economic animal feed. Another edible part of the palm tree is its fruit. Not all palms produce edible fruits, but some, such as the urucuri palm, produce fruit that is tasty. Palm cabbage is a delicacy that can only be obtained by cutting down the entire palm tree. Since this tends to be wasteful, preparing the dish is not encouraged in Haiti, where deforestation is a grave problem.

Palm Oil

Oil can be extracted not only from the seeds but also from the leaves of several varieties of palm tree. The oil is used in cooking and as a lubricant in the manufacture of many materials. Palm leaves also produce wax. The wax can be used for candles, shoe polish, lipsticks, records, and floor wax. With all these uses for palm trees, the trees are clearly an indispensable part of Haitian life.

PALM FUEL?

Palm trees may be a good source of fuel in the future. Their sap can be made into alcohol, which has the potential to be used as fuel. Palm trees that produce large amounts of sap can easily be grown in mangrove swamps and other soils unsuitable for agriculture. Haitians would benefit greatly if scientists can discover a way to use fermented palm sap as a source of fuel.

Pirates Ahoy!

In the early sixteenth century, Spain was the dominant country in the New World. France, England, and the Netherlands competed with Spain for power and influence in the region. These enemies of Spain would hire tough sailors called privateers (later shortened to pirates) to intercept Spanish ships and their cargoes of gold, silver, and gems. The pirates kept some portion of the booty and gave the remainder to the government that had hired them to conduct the raid.

Île de la Tortue

Île de la Tortue, or Tortuga Island, off Haiti's northern coast soon became an ideal haunt for pirates. The island was advantageously located along the return route back to Europe from Central and South America. It was also rocky, with many caves, perfect for hiding not only pirates and their ships, but also valuable booty. The southern coast had a natural port that could accommodate several large ships armed with up to seventy guns each.

Origin of the Word *Buccaneer*

When they were not attacking Spanish ships, the pirates relaxed on the island. Some built homes and established fields for planting crops. They collected wood for building and repairing ships.

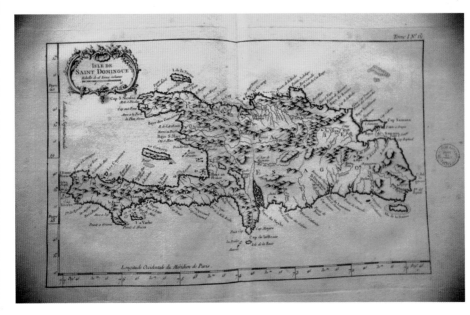

Left: **This map shows what the island of Hispaniola looked like when it was ruled by European powers from the late fifteenth century to the late eighteenth century.**

Left: **This eighteenth-century woodcut shows a vessel destroying a pirate ship in the seas off Hispaniola.**

Eventually, the pirates began crossing the 10 miles (16 km) that separated Tortuga from Hispaniola. Haiti at the time was home to herds of wild cattle and pigs. The pirates went to the mainland to hunt these animals. After the hunt, they roasted the meat over an open fire. They came to be called *boucaniers* (boo-KAH-nee-yeah), which in French means "men who barbecue." The British modified the word to *buccaneers*.

Little by little, more pirates, especially French-speaking ones, settled on the Haitian mainland. By the mid-1700s, the English and Dutch pirates had left Tortuga, and settlements on Haiti were entirely French. As more ordinary French settlers arrived on both Tortuga and the Haitian mainland, the pirates slowly became outnumbered. Most of them eventually tired of the settled, relatively safe lifestyle and drifted back to pirating and the sea.

Singing Sensations

Over the last century, Haiti has produced singers and songwriters of astounding talent and energy. Many have become famous in Haiti and overseas. Two such stars are Martha Jean-Claude and Michel Martelly.

Martha Jean-Claude was born in 1919 in Port-au-Prince, Haiti. She spent her childhood singing as a soloist at a cathedral in Port-au-Prince. In 1942, she made her professional debut at a series of folk concerts. She was exiled to Cuba by the Haitian government, and, in 1956, she released her first album, *Songs of Haiti*.

Jean-Claude's musical style draws from her deep knowledge of Haitian folklore and is faithful to Haiti's most indigenous styles of music. Her second album, *Martha Sings to the Children*, was not released until 1971; however, it was just as popular and well received as her first. Her continued exile seemed only to enhance her love for her Haitian roots, and she sang many songs

Below: **Won G (*left*) and Wyclef Jean (*right*) are two Haitian singers who have become internationally famous in recent years.**

Above: **Lauryn Hill is part of the pop group the Fugees, to which Haitian singer Wyclef Jean also belongs.**

sympathizing with the poor of Haiti and their sufferings under the Duvaliers. She returned to Haiti after the Duvalier regime ended in 1986. Her last major performance in Haiti was in 1995. She died in November 2001 at the age of 82.

Michel Martelly

Michel Martelly, known as Sweet Micky, was born in Port-au-Prince in 1961. He brings a great deal of passion and energy to the Haitian style of music known as compas. In 1989, he released his first album, *Ou la la*, to wide acclaim. His popularity continued to increase as he cultivated an image of someone who enjoys the good things in life, a lifestyle that appeals to the many people in Haiti seeking escape from their everyday hardships.

In 1994, Martelly released his second album, *I Don't Care*, which cemented his status as a rising star. He has also shown a desire to use his influence to do good. He has participated in the filming of an educational video that discusses the prevention of the human immunodeficiency virus (HIV) that causes AIDS.

The Taino

When Christopher Columbus landed on the island of Hispaniola in 1492, he was not stepping foot on uninhabited territory. A flourishing civilization of people known as the Taino had already been established on the island for hundreds of years. At the time of Columbus, in fact, the island of Hispaniola had several different Taino kingdoms.

An Ancient Lifestyle

The Taino generally were gentle, friendly people. They lived in a well-organized, hierarchical society that was divided into different groups, each one led by a dominant male called a *cacique* (kah-SEEK). They practiced polygamy, and most men had two or three wives. The cacique, however, could have as many as thirty wives.

Left: **This detailed woodcut, made in a European style characteristic of the colonial era, shows a Taino couple from the early sixteenth century.**

The Taino grew crops, including cassava, squash, and peanuts, on a large mound called a *conuco* (ko-NOO-ko). They packed the conuco with leaves to protect it from soil erosion and planted a variety of seeds to ensure that at least something would grow no matter what the weather. The Taino also raised cotton and tobacco, which they often smoked as part of their religious ceremonies.

Above: **This illustration depicts the first meeting between the Taino and the Spanish at the end of the fifteenth century.**

Taino Villages and Homes

Ordinary Taino lived in circular buildings with poles providing the primary support. These structures were covered in woven straw and palm leaves. The caciques lived in rectangular houses with porches. The houses generally were grouped in a semicircle around a flat court in the center of the village. The court was used for games and various religious and secular festivals.

The End of the Taino

The peaceful Taino people were not prepared for the full-scale invasion of their homes and lives that took place after Columbus's arrival. They were not immune to European diseases, and many succumbed to smallpox. Others were killed by the Spanish, and those who survived were enslaved and forced by the Spanish to work in the mines or fields. Their race was quickly wiped out on the island of Hispaniola. Archaeological remains are the only remnants of their culture on the island.

THE TAINO DIET

The Taino ate birds, small mammals, and snakes for protein. They also fished and hunted ducks and turtles in the lakes and sea. The Taino who lived further inland, however, relied more on various agricultural crops and had less meat or fish in their diet.

Vodun Religion

Vodun is a West African religion that has absorbed some Roman Catholic beliefs and practices. It is more commonly called voodoo. Both names can be traced to an African word for spirit. Voodoo originated in West Africa, and its roots may go back as far as 6,000 years. In the fifteenth century, African slaves brought voodoo to Haiti. The slave owners suppressed the religion, but the slaves held onto their beliefs in an effort to retain some of their former freedom.

Family Spirits

Voodoo is basically a religion involving the worship of family spirits. The spirits, called *loua* (LOO-wah), are believed to be those of deceased ancestors from both the paternal and maternal family lines. Loua protect their descendants from misfortune. In return, families must "feed" the loua during rituals where food, drink, and gifts are offered. Another important group of loua are the

Below: **Some voodoo ceremonies are colorful affairs with much music and dancing.**

various minor spirits. Some of these include *Agwe* (AH-gway), the spirit of the sea; *Aida Wedo* (ah-YEE-dah WAY-doh), the spirit of the rainbow; *Erinle* (ay-RIN-lay), the spirit of the forests; and *Zaka* (ZAH-kah), the spirit of agriculture.

Voodoo Ceremonies

Voodoo has priests and designated temples where ceremonies are performed. Major components of a voodoo ceremony include a feast beforehand and shaking a rattle, playing drums, and chanting and dancing. The priest oversees the ceremony and works to "communicate" with specific louas.

For the loua, two kinds of services are held; one is held once a year, and the other is held once a generation. Many poor families, however, wait until they have a particularly dire situation with which they need help before performing any service. Sometimes, the loua become displeased, and it is commonly believed that they show their displeasure by making people sick. Thus, voodoo rituals are often used to diagnose and treat illnesses. Performing elaborate funerals and mourning rites and making ornate tombs also help to keep the spirits of deceased family members happy.

Women in Haiti

Women in Haiti perform various roles. Rural women help a great deal with farming, and husbands often share the profits from agriculture evenly with their wives. Many rural women also travel regularly to the market to sell food or handicrafts. They do not have to share income from their sales with their husbands.

Well-educated and motivated women have an even better chance of becoming financially independent. In cities, they can work for corporations and businesses. In rural areas, women are heavily involved in petty trading and commerce.

Haitian women have worked outside the home not because of any early recognition of gender equality in Haiti. It was simply because Haiti has had rulers who realized that letting women work increased the labor force and profits. For many years, however, working women were not allowed to keep what they earned.

Woman Power
Throughout the decades, Haitian women have shown themselves to be strong and capable of taking action when necessary. For example, women's groups were instrumental in raising objections

Left: **These women work as vacation consultants at a large travel agency. Many Haitian women living in Port-Au-Prince work for large companies.**

Above: **Women in Jacmel gather in the market to sell items ranging from fruits and chickens to clothes and baskets.**

to the U.S. occupation of Haiti between 1915 and 1934. More women's groups continued to form over the next few decades. They campaigned strongly for the rights of women and children. In the mid 1940s, women's groups successfully campaigned to allow girls to attend the all-male high school system. They also obtained constitutional changes that validated women's rights. These steps helped women obtain the right to vote in the 1950s. In 1982, a decree was passed giving women all the same rights and privileges as men.

Despite improvements to their lives, women in Haiti still face obstacles today. A man may have as many wives as he wants, while a woman must remain faithful to her husband. A woman caught committing adultery faces imprisonment, while a man guilty of domestic violence against his wife may go unpunished. More changes to improve the lives of Haitian women are needed, but the perseverance and strength shown by Haitian women has helped them earn lifestyle choices enjoyed by few women in other developing countries.

RELATIONS WITH NORTH AMERICA

Haiti's relationship with North America stretches back to the end of the eighteenth century. The birth of the United States and Haiti stemmed from the desire of both countries to live free from the tyranny and oppression of colonialism.

During the 1700s, Haitians showed a deep interest in America's struggle against the British. Some of Haiti's founding fathers, such as Henri Christophe, even fought on the side of freedom in the American War of Independence. These early Haitians and Americans were clearly linked in their desire to end colonial oppression. In 1776, America became independent

Opposite: **A man in Port-au-Prince sells T-shirts that feature an image of an American dollar bill.**

from Britain; Haiti's independence came twenty-eight years later in 1804. Haiti became the second-oldest republic in the Western Hemisphere, after the United States.

Today, as Haiti moves toward democracy, it relies on the United States and Canada for aid. North American aid agencies have been very active in Haiti, while Haitian music and culture are widely appreciated in North America.

At times, Haiti's northern neighbors have not approved of the state of the country, but Haiti and its North American neighbors enjoy mutually beneficial relations today.

Above: **Haitians in the United States protest against the U.S. veto of commercial loans to Haiti. These loans are intended to improve education, health care, and other infrastructure in Haiti.**

History of U.S. Relations

During the early years of its existence as a free, black nation, Haiti was largely isolated because of the rest of the world's attitude toward slavery. The United States in particular refused to acknowledge Haiti as a country for fear that Haiti would encourage a slave rebellion within U.S. borders. After the Civil War, however, the United States recognized Haiti and began to watch the country closely because of its key location.

In the early 1900s, the United States was concerned with German influence in the Caribbean. The start of World War I led the United States to occupy Haiti in 1915. The United States set up a government and took charge of the country's economy and development.

The U.S. Occupation of Haiti (1915–1934)

The U.S. occupation had several positive effects on Haiti. Roads were improved and expanded, several towns gained access to clean water, public health improved, and Haiti's finances were well managed. But most Haitians greatly resented the U.S. intrusion. Many Haitians were poorly treated by U.S. troops, and, at one point, Haitians organized an uprising that eventually left two thousand Haitians dead.

JOHN JAMES AUDUBON (1785–1851)

John James Audubon (*above*) was born in Haiti in 1785. He left Haiti for France at an early age but carried with him the Caribbean love of nature. In France, he began learning to paint and draw. In 1803, Audubon went to the United States. From 1819 to 1839, he attempted to record in watercolor every species of North American bird he saw. He managed to capture some 489 species. After his death, people dedicated to studying and preserving bird species of North America formed the Audubon Society. It still exists today, with branches in nearly every U.S. state.

Left: A black-and-white illustration depicts the slave uprising that eventually led to Haiti's independence.

U.S. PRESIDENTS AND HAITI

Only two U.S. presidents have ever visited Haiti. Franklin Roosevelt visited Haiti in July 1934. More than sixty years later, Bill Clinton visited Haiti in March 1995.

Left: American medical workers perform surgery at a hospital in Haiti in the early part of the twentieth century.

By 1930, the United States had become concerned about the negative effects of the occupation on both Haiti and the United States. A U.S. presidential committee recommended that Haiti be allowed to govern itself. When the United States left in 1934, Haiti was only slightly better off than before. The United States had also failed to make Haiti a self-sufficient country.

The Duvalier Era (1957–1986)

In the 1960s, Haiti's close proximity to communist Cuba sparked U.S. interest in the country once again. The U.S. government began sending monetary aid to Haiti, occasionally halting the aid when it disapproved of François Duvalier's policies. The United States had halted nearly all monetary aid to Haiti by the time Jean-Claude Duvalier came to power in 1971.

In the 1970s, Jean-Claude faced pressure from the United States to change the dictatorial regime instituted by his father. He made a show of introducing some reforms, but his rule did not differ substantially from the corruption and tyranny of his father. In 1986, following strong public protests against his rule, Jean-Claude fled Haiti for France. The U.S. government played an important role in convincing him to leave the country.

Above: Frederick Douglass (1817–1895) was one of the most prominent American antislavery leaders of the nineteenth century. He served as minister to Haiti from 1889-1891.

Sanctions and Operation Uphold Democracy

Between February 1986 and March 1990, Haiti was ruled by three military-led governments, each of which was overthrown amid coups and violent antigovernment protests. In December 1990, the first fully free elections in Haiti took place, and Roman Catholic priest Jean-Bertrand Aristide won the presidency by a landslide majority. Aristide took office in early 1991, but he was deposed and exiled by yet another coup in September of that year.

Following the 1991 coup, the United States imposed a trade embargo on Haiti. President Bill Clinton increased the economic sanctions after he was elected in 1992. These economic sanctions, however, failed to convince Haiti's military rulers to return the country to democracy. Meanwhile, certain U.S. human rights groups and government officials began advocating the use of force to topple Haiti's military regime.

By August 1994, the United States had issued a clear warning to the Haitian military government: leave voluntarily or face the prospect of a U.S. invasion. The United Nations had already passed a resolution allowing the use of all necessary means to remove Haiti's military rulers and reinstate Aristide as president.

Below: **A voter leaves a polling station in Port-au-Prince after voting in the 2000 elections. The United States claims that there were irregularities in the results and has since blocked all monetary loans to Haiti.**

Left: **A Haitian in the United States raises a placard at a protest in Florida in 2001. He was protesting against the U.S. government's veto of much-needed loans to Haiti.**

Those were the objectives of Operation Uphold Democracy, which began in September 1994, when the United States began deploying troops in Haiti. The Haitian rulers, fearful of the impending invasion, quickly agreed to leave the country. As a result, the U.S. military peacefully entered Haiti and oversaw the transition to civilian government in October 1994, when Aristide was reinstated as president of Haiti.

United States-Haiti Trade Relations

The United States is Haiti's largest trading partner. Haitian exports to the United States include manufactured goods, coffee, handicrafts, essential oils, cocoa, and agricultural products such as sugar and mangoes. Haiti imports a variety of goods from the United States, including foodstuffs, machinery and transportation equipment, and petroleum.

Canada-Haiti Trade Relations

Haiti shares a special bond with Canada, the only other French-speaking country in the Western Hemisphere. Canada has been a major contributor of monetary aid to Haiti. Canada regularly trades with Haiti. Canadian imports from Haiti include apparel, copper products, fish and crustaceans, cocoa, and fruit. Major Canadian exports to Haiti include food products, paper cartons and boxes, and iron and steel products.

Haitians in the United States

The United States is home to over two million Haitian immigrants and Americans of Haitian ancestry. New York City has the second-largest community of Haitian-Americans living in the United States. The largest community of Haitian-Americans is in Florida. Other Haitian-American communities can be found in Boston and Chicago.

Haitians have been immigrating to the United States since at least the 1930s. The 1960s saw a large group of Haitians leaving the country for the United States. Another wave of Haitian immigrants came in the late 1970s and early 1980s. These Haitians were trying to escape the cruelty and corruption of the Duvalier regime. After the 1991 coup, yet another wave of frustrated Haitians sought refuge in the United States. Now that democracy has been restored in Haiti, immigration has tapered off slightly.

Haitians are making their influence felt in Florida. South Florida's Dade County is called "Little Haiti" and is considered the symbolic heart of the Haitian community in the United States. Many Haitians in Florida are registered voters. Some of them are talented and ambitious politicians. A decade ago, there were no elected Haitian-American officials in South Florida. Today, there are just under a dozen, including the mayor of North Miami, Joe Celestin, who is also the first African-American mayor of North Miami. Other Haitian-Americans who serve on the North Miami city council include Ossmann Desir and Jacques Despinosse.

Below: **Many Haitian professionals have fled Haiti for the United States in the last forty years. Once in the United States, however, it is often difficult for them to find jobs. This Haitian immigrant contemplates his future in his new homeland.**

Left: **Joe Celestin (*standing second from right*) is the first African-American mayor of North Miami, Florida. He was born in Haiti. Here he is being congratulated by supporters after being sworn in as mayor in May 2001.**

Left: **Bruny Surin (***first from right***) is a Haitian-Canadian sprinter who was born in Cap-Haïtien, Haiti. He emigrated to Canada as a child and today is one of Canada's top athletes. Here he races past Britain's Darren Campbell (***left***) and Ato Bolton (***center***) of the United States at a race in the United Kingdom in 2000.**

Haitians in Canada

Canada also has become home to many Haitian immigrants in recent decades. Many Haitians who settle in Canada are well-educated professionals who speak French. They find it easy to fit in with Canada's large French-speaking population. Over 90 percent of all Haitian-Canadians live in the province of Quebec, and Montreal has the largest community of Haitian-Canadians. Ottawa and Toronto also have large numbers of Haitian-Canadians.

Canada has benefited in many ways from these skilled, French-speaking immigrants. The large-scale arrival of Haitian doctors, nurses, teachers, and journalists to Canada coincided with Quebec's "Quiet Revolution." This was a revolution against the growth of American and English-speaking economic and cultural interests in Quebec. This growth was at the expense of French-Canadian culture. Haitian immigrants bolstered the number of French-speaking Quebecois. Today, Haitian-Canadians in Quebec are seen as an important force that helps keep French-Canadian culture and the French language alive and well.

Haitian-Canadians also preserve their Creole heritage through drama and folklore groups. Community newspapers and radio programs help the community stay in touch with its roots. One famous Haitian-Canadian is world-class sprinter Bruny Surin. Surin was born in Cap-Haïtien, Haiti, and moved to Canada when he was seven years old. He has represented Canada at many competitions, including the Olympic Games.

North Americans in Haiti

The United States has played an important role in providing economic aid and humanitarian assistance to Haiti since the beginning of the twentieth century. The United States Peace Corps also sends volunteers to Haiti. These volunteers assist Haitians in various fields, including the development of small businesses, the provision of medical services and vaccinations, food distribution, agricultural training, and environmental awareness training. More than three hundred Peace Corps volunteers have served in Haiti, and this volunteer program has been important in building people-to-people links between Haiti and the United States.

Canadian aid agencies such as the Canadian International Development Agency are also active in sending economic and humanitarian contributions to Haiti. Canada sends food, money, and volunteers. Canadian law enforcers also have been sent to Haiti as volunteers to help teach the Haitian police force law enforcement techniques. Several Canadian church groups assist development work in Haiti. Some of these groups provide Haitians with solar ovens and teach them how to use the ovens.

Below: An American woman helps feed an infant in a hospice for terminally ill children in Port-au-Prince. The hospice, situated in one of the poorest slums of the city, receives funds from American donors.

Since a democratic government has been established in Haiti, American-owned businesses have opened there. These businesses include banks, airlines, and assembly plants. Large North American companies that operate in Haiti include Citibank, American Express, American Airlines, and the Bank of Nova Scotia. A Haitian-American Chamber of Commerce also has been set up in Port-au-Prince to encourage business between the two countries.

Port-au-Prince is also home to a number of American schools and cultural institutes, including the New American School, the American Academy, and the Haitian American Institute. These centers act as focal points where Haitians and Americans can meet to exchange ideas and gain information.

Above: **Haitian girls hold hands as they walk to church in Port-de-Paix. Churches in Canada and the United States regularly donate money to charities in Haiti. North American parishes also send volunteers to assist with development projects in Haiti.**

Tourism

Many North Americans travel to Haiti. Tourism is an important part of Haiti's economy and most of Haiti's tourists come from North America. Haiti enjoys good weather, and North Americans are free to visit any time of the year to enjoy sunny weather, low prices, and a vibrant and colorful culture.

Haiti and the Harlem Renaissance

The Harlem Renaissance was an African-American cultural movement that emerged in the 1920s and early 1930s. The movement was centered in the Harlem neighborhood of New York City. This cultural movement marked the first time that the general public in the United States began to notice African-American art, literature, theater, and music.

Some of the leaders of the Harlem Renaissance were deeply influenced by the history of Haiti. For artists like Eugene O'Neill, Paul Robeson, and Charles Gilpin, Haiti represented the notion that people of African descent can determine the course of their own history. O'Neill's 1920 play, *The Emperor Jones*, is based on the life of Henri Christophe. Two major off-Broadway plays, *Black Macbeth* (1936) produced by John Houseman and directed by Orson Welles and William DuBois's *Haiti* (1938), also showed African Americans' fascination with Haiti's rich and colorful history. These plays made audiences think about issues ranging from slavery to freedom and independence and from the ability of people to govern themselves to the abuse of power.

Below: **Jacob Lawrence (1917–2000) was one of America's leading African-American artists and has painted historical and political events of Haiti.**

Left: **Haitian-American actress Garcelle Beauvais (*left*) poses with actor Michael Clark Duncan (*right*) at a film premier in Los Angeles, California. Beauvais has acted with Will Smith in the movie *Wild Wild West* (1999) and has appeared on the hit television series *NYPD Blue*.**

One African-American artist who was profoundly inspired by DuBois's play *Haiti* was painter Jacob Lawrence. In 1937, Lawrence began to paint the *Toussaint L'Ouverture* series, a collection of panels depicting the life and deeds of François Toussaint L'Ouverture. The paintings also highlight many issues connected with Haitian history, including colonialism, European expansionism, plantation economies, and the slave trade. These panels were based on both historical and fictional accounts of Haiti's history. The whole series of forty-one panels was unveiled in 1939 in Baltimore, Maryland, and was immediately praised by art critics for its bold style and lively colors. The *Toussaint L'Ouverture* series can be viewed today in the Aaron Douglas Collection, which is housed at Tulane University's Amistad Research Center in New Orleans, Louisiana.

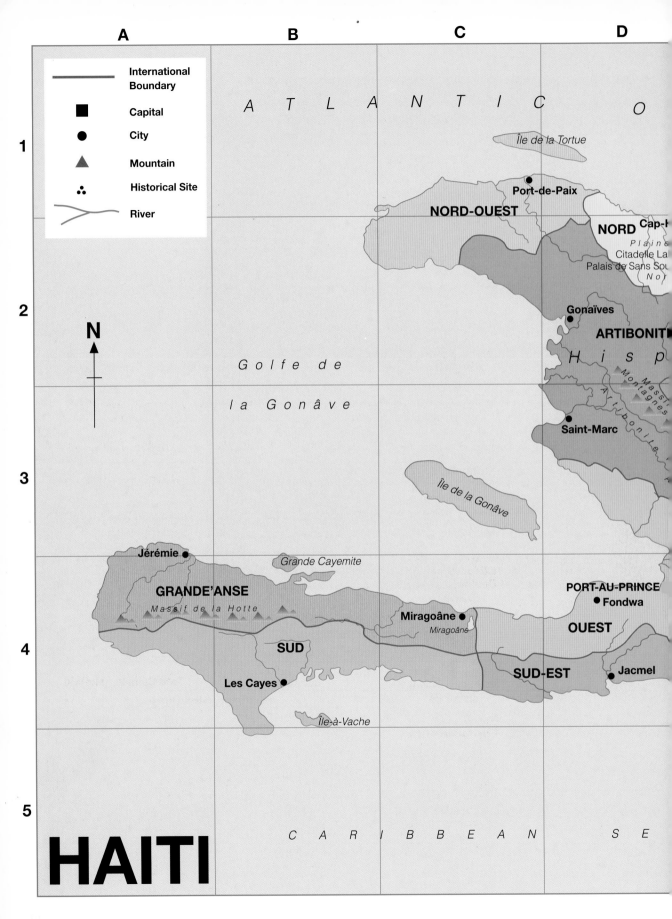

A   **B**   **C**   **D**

International
Boundary

Capital

City

Mountain

Historical Site

River

1

A T L A N T I C   O

Île de la Tortue

Port-de-Paix

NORD-OUEST

NORD Cap-H

Plaine
Citadelle La
Palais de Sans Sou
Nor

2

N

Golfe de

Gonaïves

ARTIBONIT

H i s p

la Gonâve

Massif
Montagnes
Artibonite

Saint-Marc

3

Île de la Gonâve

Jérémie

Grande Cayemite

GRANDE'ANSE

PORT-AU-PRINCE
Fondwa

Massif de la Hotte

Miragoâne

Miragoâne

OUEST

SUD

4

SUD-EST

Jacmel

Les Cayes

Île-à-Vache

5

C A R I B B E A N   S E

HAITI

86

Above: This painting by Haitian Alexandre Grégoire depicts Toussaint L'Ouverture being taken to France after his arrest by French forces.

Artibonite (department)
  C2-E3
Artibonite River D2–E3
Artibonite River Valley
  D3–E3
Atlantic Ocean A1–E1

Bonnet-à-l'Evêque D2

Cap-Haïtien D2
Caribbean Sea A5–E5
Centre (department)
  D2–E3
Citadelle LaFerrière D2
Cul-de-Sac Plain D4

Dominican Republic
  E1–E5

Étang Saumâtre
  (lake) E4

Fondwa D4
Fort Liberté E2

Golfe de la Gonâve
  B2–B3
Gonaïves D2
Grand'Anse
  (department) A3–C4
Grande Cayemite B3–B4

Hispaniola A4–E5

Île-à-Vache B4
Île de la Gonâve C3

Île de la Tortue (Tortuga
  Island) C1–D1

Jacmel D4
Jérémie A3

Les Cayes B4

Massif de la Hotte
  (mountains) A4–B4
Massif des Montagnes
  Noires (mountains)
  D2–D3
Milot D2
Miragoâne C4
Miragoâne (lake) C4

Nord (department) D1–E2
Nord-Est (department)
  E2–E3

Nord-Ouest (department)
  B2–D2

Ouest (department)
  C3–E4

Palais de Sans Souci D2
Pic la Selle E4
Plaine du Nord D2
Port-au-Prince D4
Port-de-Paix C1

Saint-Marc D3
Saut d'Eau E3
Sud (department)
  A4–C4
Sud-Est (department)
  C4–E5

Trou Caiman (lake) E4

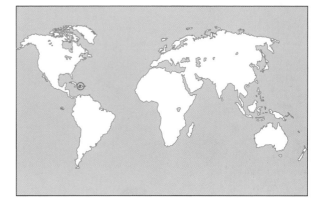

E

Fort-Liberté
à-l'Evêque
eet/900 m)

NORD-EST

i o l a

CENTRE

d'Eau

Valley

tang
umâtre

Pic la Selle
(8,793 feet/ 2,680 m)

DOMINICAN REPUBLIC

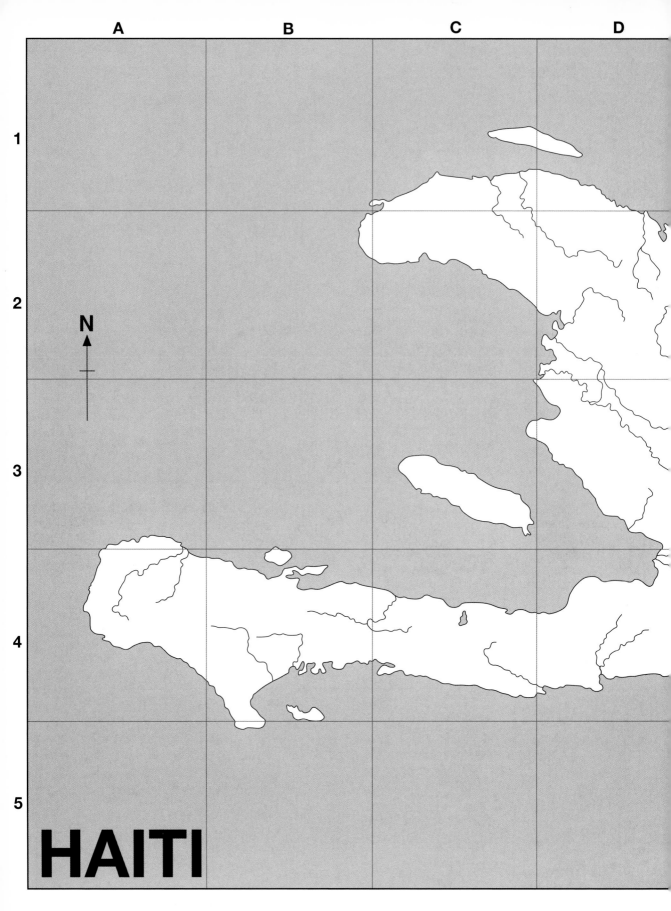

A B C D

1

2

N

3

4

5

HAITI

E

Above: **Haitians in Port-au-Prince cram into a colorful tap-tap.**

How Is Your Geography?

Learning to identify the main geographical areas and points of a country can be challenging. Although it may seem difficult at first to memorize the locations and spellings of major cities or the names of mountain ranges, rivers, deserts, lakes, and other prominent physical features, the end result of this effort can be very rewarding. Places you previously did not know existed will suddenly come to life when referred to in world news, whether in newspapers, television reports, other books and reference sources, or on the Internet. This knowledge will make you feel a bit closer to the rest of the world, with its fascinating variety of cultures and physical geography.

Used in a classroom setting, the instructor can make duplicates of this map using a copy machine. (PLEASE DO NOT WRITE IN THIS BOOK!) Students can then fill in any requested information on their individual map copies. Used one-on-one, the student can also make copies of the map on a copy machine and use them as a study tool. The student can practice identifying place names and geographical features on his or her own.

Haiti at a Glance

Official Name	Republic of Haiti
Capital	Port-au-Prince
Official Languages	Haitian Creole and French
Population	6,964,549 (2001 estimate)
Land Area	10,641 square miles (27,560 square km)
Departments	Artibonite, Centre, Grand'Anse, Nord, Nord-Est, Nord-Ouest, Ouest, Sud, Sud-Est
Highest Point	Pic la Selle 8,793 feet (2,680 m)
Coastline	1,100 miles (1,770 km)
Major Cities	Cap-Haïtien, Gonaïves, Port-au-Prince
Major River	Artibonite
Major Lakes	Étang Saumâtre, Miragoâne, Trou Caiman
Major Festivals	Independence Day (January 1)
	Carnival (February/March)
	Easter (March/April)
	Christmas Day (December 25)
Famous Leaders	François Toussaint L'Ouverture (c. 1743–1803), Jean-Jacques Dessalines (c. 1758–1806), Henri Christophe (1767–1820), François Duvalier (1907–1971), Jean-Claude Duvalier (1951–)
National Anthem	"La Dessalinienne"
Major Exports	Cocoa, coffee, oils, mangoes
Major Imports	Food, fuels, machinery, transportation equipment, petroleum products
Currency	Gourde (HTG 27.11 = U.S. $1 as of 2002)

Opposite: **Women traders offer vegetables for sale along a Port-au-Prince street.**

Glossary

Haitian Vocabulary

Agwe (AH-gway): the sea spirit in the voodoo religion.

Aida Wedo (ah-YEE-dah WAY-doh): the spirit of the rainbow in the voodoo religion.

bamboche (bum-BAWSH): a weekly party held on Saturday evenings, when families and friends gather to eat, drink, dance, and tell stories.

borlette (bore-LET): the local street-corner lottery in Haiti.

boucaniers (boo-KAH-nee-yeah): literally the French word for "men who barbecue"; pirates who lived on Île de la Tortue and the Haitian mainland who also supported themselves by hunting and farming; the origin of the English word *buccaneers*.

bwa seche (BWAH sash): literally the French word for "dry wood"; used in telling riddles when a person is not able to answer a riddle.

cacique (kah-SEEK): the male leader of a group of Taino people.

compas (KOM-pah): a type of popular Haitian music that combines jazz, merengue, and rock and roll with voodoo drumbeats.

conuco (ko-NOO-ko): a large mound on which the Taino planted many crops, one on top of the other.

Erinle (ay-RIN-lay): the forest spirit in the voodoo religion.

gagé (GAH-zhay): the pit in which cockfights take place.

griot (GREE-yoh): a popular meat dish made with either mutton or pork. The meat is first boiled, then fried and served with a very spicy sauce called *ti-malice*.

klorat (CLAW-raht): a special type of firework set off by children during Christmas celebrations.

lakou (lah-KOOH): the extended family group consisting of aunts, uncles, cousins, in-laws, and grandparents.

lambi (LOM-bee): a dish of fresh conch in a savory garlic sauce.

loua (LOO-wah): voodoo spirits; includes the spirits of deceased family members and other minor spirits.

marrons (MAH-ron): runaway slaves.

mizik rasin (mee-ZIHK rah-SEEN): also called roots music; a style of Haitian music popular in Haiti and abroad.

pain patate (pahn pah-TAHT): a delicious dessert cake made with potatoes, coconuts, and raisins.

plasaj (plah-SAHJ): a type of common-law marriage practiced by the lower classes in Haiti. It does not involve a civil or church ceremony.

ra-ra (RAH-rah): bands of musicians and singers that roam the streets during Lenten and Easter celebrations. Band members wear colorful costumes.

riz djon-djon (ree JON-JON): a rice dish cooked with small black mushrooms.

riz pois collés (ree pwah KUHL-lay): a dish of rice and red beans.

tap-tap (tup-TUP): a colorful bus used for public transportation and commonly seen on the streets of Port-au-Prince.

tim tim (teem TEEM): the words spoken by a person who wants to tell a riddle.

ti-malice (tee-MAH-liss): the hot sauce that forms part of a dish called *griot*.

Tonton Macoutes (tohn-tohn mah-KOOT): François Duvalier's rural militia group that eliminated opposition to his rule.

vodun (voh-DAHN): the religion in Haiti that is practiced by nearly all Haitians, including Christians. It is more popularly known as voodoo.

Zaka (ZAH-kah): the spirit of agriculture in the voodoo religion.

English Vocabulary

amenities: facilities that provide comfort or convenience.

anticipation: the act of waiting or expecting.

azure: the blue color of a clear sky.

booty: treasure illegally captured from a ship.

concerted: performed by agreement.

conch: a mollusk.

coup: a sudden, often violent, overthrow of a government.

desertification: the processes by which an area becomes a desert.

embezzle: use or take money that is not one's own.

endemic: natural to or characteristic of a particular place.

entrenched: firmly established.

idyllic: charmingly simple and rustic.

indigenous: originating in or characteristic of a particular region or country.

indispensable: cannot do without.

infrastructure: a country's basic facilities, including industry, education, health care, transportation, and telecommunications.

lubricant: oil; grease.

lucrative: profitable.

manatees: plant-eating aquatic mammals, also called sea cows.

merengue: a ballroom dance of Dominican and Haitian origin, characterized by a stiff-legged, limping step.

militia: a group of soldiers made up of ordinary citizens.

mulattoes: people who have one parent of European ancestry and one parent of African ancestry.

nuclear family: a social unit consisting of a father, a mother, and their children.

outlandish: strange and bizarre.

paternalistic: managed in the manner of a father dealing benevolently and often harshly with his children.

plantains: tropical fruits resembling bananas.

posh: stylish and elegant.

potable: fit for drinking.

purgatives: medicines that cause the bowels to empty.

repressive: restricting; limiting and suppressing.

republic: a government in which the people elect representatives who govern according to law.

squandered: wasted.

tenure: period or term in political office.

trade winds: winds that blow steadily toward the equator in most of the world's tropical and subtropical regions.

More Books to Read

Crisis in Haiti. Headliners series. Meish Goldish (Millbrook Press)

Haiti. Countries and Cultures series. Kerry A. Graves (Bridgestone Books)

Haiti. Countries: Faces and Places series. Elma Schemenauer (Child's World)

Haiti. Countries of the World series. Suzanne Paul Dell'Oro (Bridgestone Books)

Haiti. Cultures of the World series. Roseline NgCheong-Lum (Benchmark Books)

Haiti. Enchantment of the World series. Martin Hintz (Children's Press)

Haiti. Major World Nations series. Suzanne Anthony (Chelsea House)

Haiti. Modern Nations of the World series. Emily Wade Will (Lucent Books)

Haiti: Land of Inequality. World in Conflict series. Mary C. Turck (Lerner)

A Haitian Family. Journey between Two Worlds series. Keith Elliot Greenberg (Lerner)

Taste of Salt: A Story of Modern Haiti. Frances Temple (HarperTrophy)

Toussaint L'Ouverture, Lover of Liberty. Laurence Santrey (Troll Association)

Videos

Haiti: A Painted History. (Home Vision Cinema)

Haiti: Waters of Sorrow. Cousteau 2 series. (Turner Home Entertainment)

Web Sites

haiti.uhhp.com

windowsonhaiti.com/index.html

www.discoverhaiti.com

www.doitcaribbean.com/haiti/

www.haiti.org

www.webster.edu/~corbetre/haiti/haiti.html

Due to the dynamic nature of the Internet, some web sites stay current longer than others. To find additional web sites, use a reliable search engine with one or more of the following keywords to help you locate information about Haiti. Keywords: *François Duvalier, Palais de Sans Souci, Tonton Macoutes, Toussaint L'Ouverture, vodun.*

Index